THE I

by
Fernando Cervantes

*All booklets are published thanks to the
generous support of the members of the
Catholic Truth Society*

CATHOLIC TRUTH SOCIETY
PUBLISHERS TO THE HOLY SEE

Contents

Introduction

The Inquisition is undoubtedly one of the most readily available excuses for distrusting the Catholic Church. The very word *inquisitio* - first developed in the twelfth century as a legal term to describe a supervisory authority that investigated and judged suspected heretics - has become almost synonymous with obscurantist bigotry, intolerance, and cruelty. A "wild monster, of such strange form and horrible mien that all Europe trembles at the mere mention of its name", wrote the Portuguese Jew Samuel Usque in the early sixteenth century.[1] A "dreadful engine of tyranny" which "may at any time be introduced into a country where the Catholics have the ascendancy" and where "all laws and institutions are sacrificed to satiate the most bigoted vengeance", wrote John Foxe some decades later.[2]

This attitude has been remarkably resilient. It emerges with predictable relish even in various historical accounts that claim to base themselves on factual evidence and careful documentary research. When the American

---

[1] Quoted in David Raphael (ed.) *The Expulsion 1492 Chronicles* (Hollywood, 1992), p. 136.
[2] *The Book of Martyrs* (London, 1863 edn), p. 153.

historian John Motley wrote his classic history of the Dutch Republic, first published in 1855, for example, he referred to the Spanish Inquisition as "a bench of monks without appeal, ... judging and executing its horrible decrees without responsibility", delving into the private secrets of the "individual conscience", and practising "all the forms of torture which the devilish ingenuity of the monk had invented". "The imagination sickens", he concluded, "when striving to keep pace with these dreadful realities".[3]

Of course, modern Catholic sensibility also revolts against any notion of a society where, as Tennyson famously put it in his patriotic ballad *The Revenge*, "the thumbscrew and the stake" might be used "for the glory of the Lord". And such revulsion is by no means new among Catholics: as early as the sixteenth century various Catholic Italian ambassadors already made reference to the terror induced by the Spanish Inquisition, referring to it as a hypocritical instrument created, not for the alleged purpose of purifying the Catholic faith, but for the more obvious and expedient purpose of robbing the Jews of their wealth. Similarly, in the late eighteenth century the German Catholic Andreas Zaupser referred to the

---

[3] *The Rise of the Dutch Republic* (London, 1912 edn), p. 165.

Inquisition as a "hag", "a plague of reason and religion", and a "murderess of the mind".[4]

So there is nothing startlingly novel about Cardinal Joseph Frings's famous attack on the modern successor of the Inquisition. During one of the early sessions of the Second Vatican Council, the Cardinal referred to the secrecy and censorship that he saw at work at the heart of the Church's own central government as "a cause of scandal to the world". Interestingly, one of Cardinal Frings's chief advisers at the time was none other than Joseph Ratzinger, now Pope Benedict XVI, who, shortly afterwards, went on to join other leading theologians in a statement that lamented that the church had "reins that are too tight, too many laws, many of which have helped to leave the century of unbelief in the lurch, instead of helping it to redemption".[5]

Changes in Attitude

What was new, however, was the way in which these opinions seemed likely to overturn the age-old teaching of the Church that had for centuries insisted that error had no rights and that it was therefore the duty of Christian states

---

[4] Quoted in Christine Caldwell Ames, "Does the Inquisition Belong to Religious History?" *American Historical Review* 110.1 (February, 2005), p. 1.

[5] Quoted in Eamon Duffy, "On the Other Side", *The Times Literary Supplement* (16 December, 2005), p. 8.

to foster Catholic truth and to suppress whatever was alien to it. Indeed, when in 1965 the Second Vatican Council issued its Declaration on Religious Liberty, clearly and unequivocally stating that freedom of religious thought and practice was a fundamental human right derived from the basic dignity and freedom of every human person as a child of God, many could not help but see it as a bold and potentially damaging initiative that might cast serious doubt on the teaching authority of the Church. After all, most Catholics at that time had been taught that the notion of religious freedom was one of the poisoned fruits of the Enlightenment: a sinful affront against the immutability of revealed truth. Heretics might hope for some degree of toleration as a matter of pragmatism and prudence, but for them to expect religious freedom and equal rights was tantamount to expecting the Church to accept that the truth was relative and that error had rights.

It is not surprising that many Catholics at the time, notably Archbishop Marcel Lefebvre, saw the Declaration as an abomination: an irresponsible and illegitimate decision that broke with a millennium and a half of constant Christian tradition. Yet the Church has not wavered. Every pontiff since the Council has acknowledged that the unfortunate history of involvement of the Church in persecution has discredited her in the eyes of the world and will continue to hinder her efforts to proclaim the dignity of every human person as redeemed by Christ. There can be no question about Pope John Paul II's deep concern for this issue. In his 1994 encyclical letter, *Tertio Millennio Adveniente*, he exhorted Catholics to enter the new millennium with a clear awareness of their history, urging them to repent of "past errors and instances of infidelity, inconsistency and lack of courage". Among these, the Pope specifically singled out the history of religious persecution. Accordingly, in the Autumn of 1998, the world's leading historians of the Inquisition were invited to a symposium at the Vatican to assist the Church in a solemn act of "purification of memory in penitence" after confronting her own persecuting past. They were asked to present a collective picture of the history of the Inquisition in the presence of a theological commission that would then prepare a reflection for the Pope as the basis for an "apology" - rather like the apology for the Shoah that he had published the previous year.

John Paul II's 'Apology'

The unease felt by many of those present is not difficult to understand; for the theological commission worked strictly in line with the brief that John Paul II had set in *Tertio Millennio Adveniente*, where the Pope had carefully avoided any mention of the need for the institutional Church to repent, writing instead about "the children of the Church". This subtle distinction was echoed during the symposium by the distinguished French theologian J. M. Garrigues, who proposed that the undeniable fact that the *magisterium* of the Church had been "silent" on the issue of religious freedom until the Second Vatican Council's declaration of 1965 did not in itself affect the Church's doctrinal authority. In other words, Garrigues proposed that although there could be no question that the implicit justification of religious persecution during the last millennium and a half was abhorrent to the Gospel and should be repudiated, this was not to say that the doctrinal authority of the institutional Church had been in any way directly implicated in the process.

Many of those present, and the bulk of popular public opinion, found this argument unconvincing. Surely, if the Inquisition had been established and given special privileges by a long list of Popes, some of whom had also promulgated official bulls against heresy and witchcraft which condoned persecution and even death in cases of recalcitrance, there could be no question that the institutional Church was directly implicated in this shameful history. As the distinguished Jewish historian Carlo Ginzburg explained: in the face of these blatant facts, any papal "apology" for the Inquisition would ring as hollow as the 1997 "apology" for the Shoah, since it would amount to an evasion of responsibility. How, after all, could the dead forgive? He would much rather hear the Pope and the Church state clearly and unambiguously that they were *ashamed* of the Inquisition, instead of asking for an easy absolution that could not be given.

Significantly, it was not just those who were critical of the Church's past involvement in religious persecution who were loath to hear the Pope asking for an easy absolution. Many of the critics of John Paul II's decision to apologise for the Inquisition came from conservative and traditional sectors. They saw the initiative as a naïve capitulation to the wishes of more progressive sectors who wished to see the Church acknowledge that the "structural sin" that the Pope himself had discerned in the world's political and economic structures had always operated within the Church in very much the same way. Even more worrying to some was the implicit acknowledgement in any such "apology" that the distorted historical interpretations of the Church's involvement in religious persecution, especially those referring to the Inquisition, were historically accurate accounts, when, in a good number of cases, they could be shown to be largely the result of prejudice and propaganda.

The question is therefore more complex than it appears at first sight, and it is clear that it cannot be adequately addressed without some knowledge of the historical circumstances that led to the various justifications of religious violence in the history of the Church. More than ever, it would seem, there is a clear need to separate fact from fiction in the history of these movements. It is the purpose of this booklet to attempt to give some historical context to this delicate topic with specific reference to the history of the Inquisition.

The Background

As we have seen, in his address to the 1998 symposium J. M. Garrigues referred to the "silence" of the Church's *magisterium* on the issue of religious liberty. Despite arguing that this "silence" did not directly compromise the doctrinal authority of the church, Garrigues nonetheless acknowledged that it left the door open to an implicit justification of religious persecution by the Church during a millennium and a half. Significantly, Garrigues used the term "political Augustinianism" when referring to this development. We need to begin by trying to clarify what this term might mean.

"Political Augustinianism"

At first sight, the term seems to imply that much of the responsibility for the Church's implicit justification of religious violence through the centuries can be laid on St Augustine's shoulders. It is true that, in the early fifth century, the great African saint developed a characteristically persuasive argument in favour of the forced conversion of Donatists - a sectarian group of Christians who exalted the note of holiness above that of universality and who maintained that there could be no forgiveness for those who had fallen away from the Church, especially in times of persecution.

St Augustine's argument - in effect the only full justification in the history of the early Church of the right of the state to suppress non-Catholics - came as a bit of a shock. Up until then it had been practically unthinkable for a Christian to advocate a policy of persecution. Indeed, St Augustine himself had only recently expressed serious doubts about the wisdom of such an initiative in the face of the large number of feigned converts who had joined the Church *en masse* after Christianity had become the established religion of the Roman Empire. It seemed pretty clear to him, in fact, that forced conversions were more than likely to be counterproductive and to lead to resentment and hypocrisy.

The crucial turning point came when the Donatists were brought under the Roman Empire's general laws against heresy by the drastic 'Edict of Unity' in June 405. After this, St Augustine was characteristically quick to see the hand of Providence at work. To object to the imperial edict, because it was likely to provoke more feigned conversions, now seemed to him to run the danger of denying that God's grace could bring about a change of heart, even in those who had been coerced. After all, his own experience had taught St Augustine that there was an unbridgeable gulf between human circumstances and intentions on the one hand, and the invincible purpose of Divine Providence on the other. So, although he would always maintain that the final, individual act of choice had to be free in order to be effective, he also argued that, in many circumstances, such a choice needed to be prepared by processes which individuals did not necessarily choose for themselves. These processes, moreover, were often imposed on individuals against their will.

To explain his position, St Augustine compared the predicament of the coerced Donatists to that of the Israelites under the Law of Moses. The Law, he explained, had been understood and loved by a tiny minority, who, nonetheless, had imposed it on the majority by force and fear. Yet, this blatantly coercive initiative had deterred the Jews from the worse sins of polytheism; as such, it had constituted the necessary preparation for the unity of the Church that had been distilled to the Jews of Jerusalem at Pentecost. This unity, moreover, had not been reserved for the spiritual few: it had been embraced by a large number of plainly sinful people, who lived at a moral level which was perfectly comparable to that of the ancient Israelites, and who would consequently still only respond to coercion and fear.

Here in a nutshell we have the foundations of a fundamentally pessimistic view of human nature and human society, where coercion and restraint would come to play a fundamental role. Without them, St Augustine would write in a memorable passage, "no king in his kingdom, no general with his troops, ... no husband with his wife, nor father with his son, would attempt to put a stop...to the freedom and the sheer sweet taste of sinning".[6] It is just such an attitude that we find at the core of Garrigues's "political Augustinianism", an attitude that has been repeatedly used to justify force and coercion to impose the Christian faith. The frequency of appeals to his thought in order to justify such initiatives has even earned St Augustine the unenviable attribute of having been the "first theorist of the Inquisition".[7]

To be fair to him, we should remember that coercion always remained for St Augustine a genuinely corrective treatment. He would undoubtedly have been horrified at the ways in which this particular teaching has been re-interpreted and abused. At any rate, since it would take another seven centuries for the Inquisition

---

[6] Quoted in Peter Brown, *Augustine of Hippo: A Biography* (London, 1967), p. 240.

[7] See, for example, H. Maisonneuve, "Croyance religieuse et contrainte: la doctrine de S. Augustin", *Mél. de science relig.* xix, 1962, pp. 49-68.

itself to appear on the soil of Europe, it is necessary to examine the particular circumstances that led to that radically new departure.

Catharism

In the eleventh century, a new religious movement began to spread across southern Europe. By the twelfth and thirteenth centuries it had become seriously threatening to the Church. Known as Catharism (from the Greek word for purity), it is best described not so much as a heresy as a rival religion; for it did not sink its roots in Christianity, but in a view of the world that pre-dated Christianity and that was fundamentally opposed to it.

It is important to stress this point because Catharism is too often thought to be a form of simplified or rationalised Christianity, akin to the various contemporary movements of reform that had begun to advocate a return to the simplicity of the gospels and the cult of poverty. This fundamentally incorrect view has led to a widespread assumption that it is this aspect of the movement that some of the more corrupt members of the Church hierarchy found especially threatening. But nothing could be more mistaken. The real roots of the movement are in fact to be found in the pre-Christian dualism of the ancient

East, which at this time was being transmitted to Western Europe, through the Balkan peninsula, by the Bogomils and Paulicians.

Catharism was essentially a dualistic religion. It regarded the whole of the material world, and especially the human body, as the evil creation of Satan. Consequently, it was fundamentally opposed, not only to the whole sacramental system of Catholicism, but also to the most basic institutions of Christian society - especially marriage and childbearing, which it specifically condemned as obnoxiously sinful.

On the other hand, the life of strict asceticism which Catharism demanded in principle was by no means expected to be achieved by every Cathar, but only by the very few *perfecti*, or "perfect" ones - those who had received the only sacrament of the Cathar religion: the "baptism with the spirit and with fire", also known as the *consolamentum*. The others were merely *credentes* - "believers" - who could hope for no share in the privileges and the privations of the *perfecti*. And since the body was evil anyway, many in practice held that it did not matter much what one did with it so long as children were not generated in the process. Thus Catharism combined an extreme form of asceticism among a small, "pure", minority, and a considerable degree of moral laxity, often slipping into plain

antinomianism, among the great majority for whom
normal sexual intercourse between a man and a woman
was anathema.

Responding to Heresy

What made matters considerably more difficult from the
point of view of the Church was that the Cathars
recognised no diocesan boundaries. This meant that the
normal mechanisms for searching out and restraining
heresy, dependent as they were on the authority of the
bishops, were largely ineffective against them. By the late
twelfth century, moreover, the movement was spreading
well beyond its initial bases in northern Spain, southern
France, and northern Italy, and it had become seriously
threatening to the health and stability of the Christian
community. It is, therefore, hardly surprising that it was
precisely at this time that the more ruthless and intolerant
attitude to heresy that would become characteristic of the
later medieval Church began to emerge.

But there is a danger in oversimplifying the cause-and-
effect pattern of this development if some important
antecedents are not borne in mind. As we have seen, the
suppression of heresy had been regarded as part of the
duty of properly constituted Christian authorities since
the time of St Augustine. Yet the principle implicit in the
sentence *ecclesia abhorret a sanguine* - "the Church

abhors the shedding of blood" - had been consistently upheld in official circles. This remained true even after increasing numbers of rulers and bishops had begun to execute heretics from the eleventh century onwards; indeed, all such initiatives were specifically condemned by the leaders of public opinion - notably by St Bernard and by Gerhoh of Reichersberg.

The emergence of Catharism, however, brought a twofold complication to this tradition. Firstly, Catharism was no ordinary heresy, but an emphatically dualistic, and for all intents and purposes Manichean, religion. Now the Manichees had been regarded as capital enemies of humanity since pre-Christian times - indeed, Manicheism was a capital offence in Roman Law, and the Byzantine Empire had repeatedly attempted to exterminate the movement. Secondly, the emergence of Catharism happened to coincide with the moment when the Church had begun to take the lead in preaching the Crusade against the infidel abroad, a development that made it increasingly difficult - in fact, blatantly inconsistent - to condemn the shedding of blood against heretics at home.

Heresy as Treason

These are the circumstances that explain the growth of a movement in favour of a Crusade against the Cathars during the second half of the twelfth century. It culminated in the formal declaration of the Crusade against the Albigenses in 1208, an event that marked a definite shift in the treatment of heresy. It was given official sanction by Pope Innocent III's implicit assimilation of heresy to the crime of high treason (*laesae maiestatis*). This initiative was inseparable from the tendency of the Popes at this time to assume direct responsibility for the control of Christian society and it was inevitably conditioned by their long and difficult struggle with the Hohenstaufen Emperors. But it is a mistake to see it merely as an arbitrary, top-down imposition; for it was, in fact, the logical conclusion of the prevailing conception of society, which was essentially unitary and theocratic; indeed, it was this very notion that had brought the Sacred Empire itself into existence. According to it, the ultimate social unit was neither the "Church" nor the "State" (which, at any rate, are emphatically anachronistic terms when applied to the Middle Ages), but the Christian society. The struggle between Popes and Emperors was not so much one of opposition as one of precedence, for they both accepted the unitary and theocratic conception of the Christian society. This meant that whoever emerged triumphant from the struggle would face the mammoth task of governing the Christian society from a perspective in which any form of heresy would inevitably become increasingly difficult to tolerate. Now, although the penalty for high treason in Roman Law was death, it is significant that, even after Innocent III had implicitly assimilated heresy to high treason, he nonetheless remained faithful to the *ecclesia abhorret a sanguine* principle and decreed only exile and confiscation in the anti-heresy laws promulgated in the Fourth Lateran Council of 1215.

The real turning point came when Emperor Frederick II made heresy punishable by burning in 1224. It is likely that the motives behind the zeal with which Frederick opted to persecute heretics were a complex combination of an attempt to cover up his own manifestly doubtful orthodoxy, on the one hand, and a subtle ploy to assert his authority in religious matters at the expense of the Church, on the other. This was the climate in which Pope Gregory IX made the bold decision to appoint a special commission in 1231 for the purpose of ensuring that the "inquisition" of heretics remained under the authority of the Church. For all intents and purposes, therefore, 1231 may be regarded as the date of the official foundation of the Inquisition.

The Medieval Inquisition

Gregory IX did not establish the Inquisition as a distinct and separate tribunal; what he did was to appoint permanent judges who were given special powers to execute their doctrinal functions in the Pope's name. These judges were primarily, though not exclusively, Dominican and Franciscan friars who were answerable directly to the Pope: they could arrest suspects on the testimony of two witnesses who remained anonymous; both suspects and witnesses were compelled to give evidence under threat of heavy penalties; suspects found guilty of heresy had ecclesiastical penances imposed upon them which often included the wearing of a badge of shame; and those who refused to repent, as well as those who relapsed, were deemed dangerous threats to Christian society and, consequently, they were handed over (or, to use the contemporary term, they were "relaxed") to the secular authorities to be burnt at the stake.

Abuses

It is obvious that such a system often lent itself to many, often quite scandalous abuses, such as those that

characteried the earliest Inquisitors, like the Dominican
Robert le Bougre. Le Bougre had himself converted
from Catharism, but he seemed to have no qualms about
proceeding against his former coreligionists with the
merciless zeal of a fanatic, burning *en masse* nearly two
hundred *perfecti* in 1239. Additionally, since it had
become a great crime to be found assisting a heretic in
any way, many lawyers grew reluctant to act as counsel
for the defence, just in case any suspicion fell upon
them. This trend quite often placed many of the accused
in a very disadvantageous position. More regrettable
still was the decision to introduce the use of judicial
torture by the Inquisition from 1252 onwards, which
constituted a serious breach with the Church's tradition
of opposing torture since Patristic times. But by far the
most harmful development was the marked growth in
interest in the crime of witchcraft among Inquisitors, a
trend that could not contrast more sharply with the
official attitude of the Church in the early Middle Ages.
Indeed, the belief in witchcraft had been ferociously
opposed by the ecclesiastical advisors of Charlemagne
and their successors, especially Pope Nicholas I and
Agobard of Lyons, who referred to witchcraft
specifically as a relic of pagan superstition. Similarly, in
the late eleventh century, Pope Gregory VII had warned
the king of Denmark to desist from persecuting witches,

urging him instead to "turn away the wrath of God by worthy penance", rather that "provoke His anger yet further by the useless savagery that you are inflicting upon these innocent people".[8] And yet, in 1484, Pope Innocent VIII issued the extraordinary Bull *Summis Desiderantes*, under the unmistakable influence of the two leading anti-witch Inquisitors in Germany: the Dominicans Heinrich Kramer and Jacob Sprenger. They, in turn, would shortly produce the most infamous of all manuals of Inquisitors, the *Malleus Maleficarum* (Hammer of the Witches). This work emphatically endorsed the belief in the existence of witches, together with the whole range of contemporary superstitions about them - notably the grotesque idea that they were in the habit of forming sexual partnerships with demons.

Thus, at this time, the official Church hierarchy contributed substantially to the formation of a persecuting mentality across Europe. The trend would in turn lead to the deaths of tens of thousands of people over the next three centuries. It is calculated that as many as 25,000 people may have been burned as witches in Germany alone. Of course, this sorry episode is part of a much wider and more complex cultural and social movement that cut across nations and faiths, and it therefore is a

---

[8] Erich Caspar (ed.), *Das Register Gregors VII*, 2 vols. (Gerlin, 1920-55), ii, p. 498.

serious mistake to blame the official Church and the Inquisition directly for it. Yet, it is undeniable that the official backing that successive Popes and Inquisitors gave to witch beliefs was a fundamental contributor to the credibility and rapid spread of the witch-craze.

An unbalanced picture

On the other hand, it is important to underline that the common tendency to dwell on the abuses has resulted in a skewed and unbalanced picture which is in need of correction. It is not often mentioned, for instance, that as soon as Pope Gregory IX got wind of Robert le Bougre's excesses, he immediately removed him from office and imprisoned him for life; that numerous manuals produced in the fourteenth century, notably those of Bernard Gui and Nicolas Eymeric, were serious and meticulous attempts to secure justice, however flawed they might appear by modern judicial standards; and that the majority of Inquisitorial cases were overseen by conscientious ecclesiastics who followed strict procedural rules, as a result of which trials for heresy or witchcraft were generally much safer for the accused in Inquisitorial courts than in secular ones. Out of 930 sentences passed by Bernard Gui in Toulouse in the early fourteenth century, for instance, only 42 delivered the accused to the secular authorities for capital punishment

- that is, one in twenty-two. The proportions for other regions are fairly comparable. The nineteenth-century Protestant historian of the Inquisition, Henry Charles Lea, who would have been only too pleased to confirm the anti-Inquisitorial prejudices of his generation, confirmed instead the "relatively few" victims after an exhaustive study of the available documentation. Indeed, by the time of the Reformation the activities of the Inquisition had declined to such insignificance that Pope Paul III had to establish the more centralised Roman Inquisition in 1542. Subsequently, to meet the challenge of militant Protestantism, a special curial congregation - the direct ancestor of the modern Congregation for the Doctrine of the Faith - was established to oversee the Inquisition's work; and another body - the Congregation of the Index - was set up to control the censorship of books. Just like its predecessor, the Roman Inquisition handed recalcitrant heretics over to the secular authorities to be burned at the stake. But again the numbers pale into insignificance when compared with the number of victims condemned by secular courts. It is only a handful of classic cases, such as the silencing of Galileo or the burning of Giordano Bruno, that would subsequently be repeatedly used, first by Protestant and later by liberal and secular propagandists, as examples of the Catholic Church's hostility to freedom of thought.

Yet by the beginning of the seventeenth century the Roman Inquisition had largely turned its attention away from the fight against heresy and towards the elimination of magical and superstitious practices among the Catholic peasantry. After this, the use of the death penalty became exceptionally rare.

Meanwhile, of course, the Spanish Inquisition had been at work in the various kingdoms of the Iberian peninsula since the late fifteenth century and had come to be widely regarded as the unacceptable face of militant Catholicism. Its allegedly horrific methods of torture, and the veritable reign of terror that the enemies of Spain claimed that it had introduced with the specific purpose of keeping the Catholic faithful in fearful submission, have become so deeply ingrained in the European historical imagination that it is almost impossible to question them without provoking reactions of deep suspicion. Dostoevsky's portrait of the Grand Inquisitor in *The Brothers Karamazov* seems irresistibly persuasive. The great Russian novelist has Christ return to earth in early modern Spain only to be confronted, arrested and rejected by none other than Torquemada himself. The Grand Inquisitor then famously asks Christ: "Why have you come to disturb us?"

The Spanish Inquisition

Religion in the medieval Spanish Kingdoms

When the Inquisition was formally established by Pope Gregory IX, in 1231, the king of Castile and León was St Ferdinand, who famously delighted in calling himself the "king of the three religions" - "a singular claim in an increasingly intolerant age", wrote the historian Henry Kamen.[9] Indeed, medieval Spain sheltered Christians, Jews and Muslims in a remarkable religious coexistence unparalleled in the rest of western Europe. It is fascinating to observe that just at the time when England and France had taken the decision to expel their Jews (in 1290 and 1306, respectively) no comparable systematic machinery was established to deal with unbelievers in Spain, where Jews and Muslims continued to be tolerated for decades to come. This was just as well, for Spain had the largest single Jewish community in the world, and Islam had been a dominant element in the culture of most of Spain south of the river Duero since the Muslim invasion of the peninsula in 711.

---

[9] *The Spanish Inquisition: An Historical Revision* (London, 1998), p. 2.

This unique religious coexistence has often been exaggerated. It was in fact always fragile and began to show quite worrying fissures in the second half of the fourteenth century, specifically as a result of the devastating impact of the Black Death and the effects of Spain's involvement in the Hundred Years' War. The aftermath of the war had actually benefited Spain financially, with a rise in commercial, especially maritime, activity that led to a notable increase of money in circulation. Yet the failure to reinvest the money caused inflation and successive devaluations. This brought about a worrying rise in social tensions that soon began to erupt in instances of urban violence. As usual, the Jews became easy scapegoats in this process; but in Spain the problem was compounded by the sheer numbers of Jews, by their concentration in the larger urban centres, and by their enviable success as merchants, traders, artisans, financiers and doctors.

These factors help to explain the remarkable speed with which one of the most calamitous of medieval anti-Jewish pogroms spread across the peninsula in 1391. The violence began in early June around Seville, where the Archdeacon of Ecija, Ferrán Martínez, had fuelled the anti-Jewish feelings of many of his parishioners by callously affirming from the pulpit, not only that the Jews had killed Christ, but also that they had caused the

Black Death by poisoning wells and that they frequently indulged in odious and sacrilegious practices, like the desecration of hosts and the sacrificial crucifixion of children. By the middle of July, the violence had spread to many major urban centres across the peninsula, as far as Toledo in the centre and Valencia in the east. By early August, the pogrom had reached Barcelona and the Balearics, and from there it soon spread as far as Perpignan. By the middle of August it had reached León, Palencia, Burgos and Logroño in the north.

The 1391 pogrom marked a dramatic turning point. Although the violence affected many non-Jews, the openly anti-Jewish rhetoric that accompanied the movement forced many Jews out of the big cities into smaller villages and rural communities, where their activities would not be so openly resented. The majority of those who survived the pogrom and who chose to stay in the larger cities, often did so only after converting to Christianity. The enormous rise in the number of conversions after 1391 is very significant, for it demonstrates that the phenomenon cannot be understood merely as a racial problem - that is, a problem arising from anti-Semitism with all the modern, post-Holocaust connotations of that term. Indeed, it seems to have been generally accepted that once Jews became Christians the problem of violence against them

would be solved. This, in fact, had been the hope of the
most charismatic preacher of the time, the Dominican St
Vincent Ferrer, who was a formidable driving force
behind the conversions of thousands of Jews and
Muslims throughout Spain during the 1410s. It is surely
of great interest that there are no known examples of
significant anti-Jewish riots for about half-a-century
after 1391. Nevertheless, the unprecedented number of
conversions did not take long to begin to generate its
own, often even more delicate, problems.

Jews and Conversos

Perhaps the most important of these was related to the
staggering success of the *Conversos* - as Jewish converts
to Christianity were known. *Conversos* naturally
preserved many of their old Jewish contacts and
traditions, but they were now free to join the ranks of the
nobility and had begun to get many influential positions -
not least in the Church hierarchy. Consequently, the
resentment that Christians had shown against Jews in the
fourteenth century began to be directed against *Conversos*
in the fifteenth, and it would express itself all the more
bitterly because *Conversos* appeared to have usurped the
privileges and prerogatives that in the past had been the
preserve of those who now began to refer to themselves
as "Old Christians". Nor did committed Jews disappear

entirely from royal favour: as late as the campaign to conquer Granada in the 1480s and early 90s, for instance, the eminent Jew, Samuel Abulafia, was in charge of supplies for the Christian troops; and his colleagues at court included the Rabbi, Abraham Seneor, and the eminent Jewish scholar, Isaac Abravanel.

A recurring accusation made by a number of "Old Christian" writers from the middle of the fifteenth century was that the Jewish background of the *Conversos* and their various contacts with Jews made it impossible for them to be good Christians. For this reason, they argued, it was imperative for the health of the body politic to oust *Conversos* from public life and to remove them from positions of influence, especially royal and ecclesiastical offices. In response, *Converso* intellectuals chose to emphasise the doctrinal unity of the "Old" and the "New" Christians. This was an admittedly unassailable argument from a theological perspective; but it nonetheless had the unfortunate effect of implicating the Jews, especially those Jews with occupations and places of residence that put them in frequent contact with Christians, as the real source of danger to Christianity.

Violence against *Conversos*

As tensions mounted, so did instances of violence against *Conversos*. The process culminated in a number of horrific riots and massacres throughout Spain in the 1460s and 70s - just at the time of a complex civil war that had broken out over the disputed succession of Isabel of Castile, who had married Ferdinand of Aragon in 1469. Paramount in the minds of both monarchs at this time was the need for unity. So after the war was settled in Isabel's favour in 1475 - and, especially, after her visit to Seville in 1477, where the Queen heard the persuasive sermons and arguments of the Dominican Alonso de Hojeda about the dangers posed by the large number of "false" *Conversos* - the monarchs began seriously to consider the need to establish a national Inquisition.

It should be emphasised that their decision was at first tentative and rather reluctant. Their central aim was to reach a definitive solution to the *Converso* problem by focusing on the religious issue. As they saw it, only this approach could provide a basis for the safe inclusion and assimilation of *Conversos* into the body politic. This point needs to be understood clearly, because the early activities of the Spanish Inquisition are too often seen as part of a concerted campaign of racial and ethnic cleansing. Nothing could be more misleading than this assumption. The fact is that Ferdinand and Isabel desperately needed the support of both *Conversos* and Jews, and thus they went out of their way to favour them. Indeed, the monarchs had received vital financial support from Jews during the campaign against Granada. Similarly, their political support during the civil war had come primarily from the urban governing classes, among whom *Conversos* - many of whom were openly supportive of the decision to establish the Inquisition - were particularly conspicuous. *Converso* support of the Inquisition is not as surprising as it might appear at first sight; for, in just the same way as the monarchs, many a genuine *Converso* will have had high hopes that the Inquisition might punish "false" *Conversos* - or "Judaisers", as they came to be called - with fines and confiscations and bans from public offices, thereby guaranteeing genuine *Conversos* - or "New Christians" - complete and unassailable immunity from any further attacks or doubts about their full membership of the Christian society.

This was the central motive behind the formal establishment of the Inquisition by Pope Sixtus IV in 1478 at the specific request of Ferdinand and Isabel. There is plenty of evidence to suggest that, up until the early 1480s, the monarchs regarded the Inquisition as a temporary emergency measure, whose immediate purpose was to ensure religious orthodoxy in Andalusia. But it was not long before the sheer complexity of the problem began to overwhelm even those who had supported the initiative. To begin with, most of the Inquisitors appointed in the early years were not trained lawyers and they possessed a very inadequate knowledge of Jewish religious practices. They, therefore, often became easy instruments of a judicial system in which social pressures and prejudices were given too much weight. The Inquisition's acceptance of anonymous denunciations and its refusal to disclose witnesses, often made it almost impossible for the accused to prove their innocence.

Expulsion of Jews

Not surprisingly, many *Conversos*, not least those who had originally favoured the establishment of the Inquisition, began to use their considerable influence in city councils to obstruct the work of Inquisitors, thereby protecting their own property and political power. Thus, from the early 1480s, city councillors and local officials began largely to disregard Crown policy and to implement openly anti-Jewish ordinances, arguing that it was the Jews, rather than the "new Christians", that needed to be removed from positions of influence. In the process, *Conversos* managed to enlist the support of a significant proportion of "Old Christians" among urban oligarchies that were growing increasingly resentful of the continuing protection afforded to Jews by Ferdinand and Isabel - notably, the special tax exemptions and immunities that the monarchs had granted them in compensation for their financial support during the final stages of the war. From the mid 1480s, therefore, the relentless passage of anti-Jewish ordinances by city councillors throughout Spain led to a process of expulsions of Jews from increasing numbers of towns and provinces. Eventually, on 30 March 1492, barely three months after the final conquest of Granada, the monarchs themselves issued an edict ordering the departure, within three months, of all Jews in their dominions who refused to convert to Christianity.

This calamitous decision was reached in haste and it ran directly against the true interests and the previous Jewish policy of the monarchs. Even taking into account the very difficult circumstances that we have just described, it is impossible to make much sense of it outside the context of the unitary and theocratic conception of the body politic that had been central to Western European political thought since the time of Charlemagne. As we have seen, the concepts of "Church" and "State", as distinct and separate organs, are grossly anachronistic when describing medieval and early modern European societies. The ultimate social and political unit was not the "State" or the "Church", but the

Christian society - Christendom. Outside Christendom, which necessarily implied membership of the Church, there was no justice and thus no legitimate authority, whether spiritual or temporal. In this context, it is of special significance that the decree of expulsion took place shortly after the final conquest of Granada, for the event marked the final emergence of the Spanish kingdoms as fully-fledged members of the unitary Christian society. When combined with the very difficult social developments that we have analysed, it is not difficult to understand why, despite their obvious reluctance, the monarchs found no option but to agree to the decree of expulsion in 1492. In a context where membership of the Christian society was inseparable from membership of the Church, heresy and apostasy came to be seen as "infections" that threatened the health of the body politic. Accordingly, the remedies would be analogous to those used in the treatments of illnesses: bleeding, purging, and, if all else failed, amputation.

It is important to understand this point, not in order to lessen the appallingly tragic impact of a decision that left approximately 100,000 Jews with the grim prospect of converting to Christianity or leaving their homeland, but in order to avoid the common and fundamentally mistaken interpretations of the event as the result of a racial intolerance along the lines of the Holocaust. It is also important for our topic to be clear that the Inquisition had nothing directly to do with the expulsion. Although a great number of Inquisitors (many of them, incidentally, *Conversos*) were in favour of the initiative, the expulsion and its difficult implementation were strictly royal decisions. The Inquisition itself had no jurisdiction over Jews, but only over Christians. False *Conversos*, or crypto-Jews, of course, were a different matter: they were now, at least nominally, Christian. This is one of the reasons why Inquisitors were in favour of the decree of expulsion. Thereafter, their task would be rendered considerably more straightforward, because anyone found practising Judaism after 1492 was effectively a heretic and an apostate.

"To convert or to depart"

Unfortunately, the cruel dilemma faced by every Spanish Jew in 1492 - whether to convert or to depart - inevitably led to an even larger number of false conversions than had previously been the case. It is calculated that approximately 50,000 Jews left the peninsula in the 1490s, which means that the other 50,000 converted in order to stay. A good number fled to Morocco where large Jewish communities already existed under Islamic rule. Many others were welcomed by the Aragonese King of Naples, Ferrante I, who was particularly pleased to have attracted the intellectual skills of Isaac Abravanel alongside many Jewish artisans. But the bulk of them chose to accept the welcome given to them by the Ottoman Sultan, who prided himself of ruling over many religions. This pattern of emigration is clearly indicative of the stubborn reluctance of Western European kingdoms to receive Jews, mostly as a result of the generally accepted notion of the unitary and theocratic nature of the Christian society. The result was that a large majority of those who left experienced terrible misery. Many were enslaved, and there was even the odd pitiful spectacle of hapless Jews confined to rotting hulks outside ports where they were not allowed to land. It is no surprise to find that a good number of those who left chose to return to Spain and convert. Back in the peninsula, they soon became aware that even those who had chosen the land route to Portugal and Navarre had been forced to convert by the late 1490s.

It is not difficult to imagine the various injustices and abuses that this situation was likely to engender. There was now no limit to the extent of Inquisitorial jurisdiction. Any Jew living in Spain was by definition either a genuine *Converso* or a willing apostate. Of course, to the Jews the situation looked entirely different: they had returned to their homeland after an unimaginably traumatic episode in their lives and were seeking to re-establish contacts with family and friends with whom they had every reason to feel aggrieved; yet, they were now in exactly the same position as those committed crypto-Jews who had nonetheless converted in order to escape the expulsion. There is convincing evidence that many of them managed to observe a number of Jewish fast days, to avoid pork, to light the Sabbath candles, and to bury their dead in secret, while, in the home, mothers did their best to transmit some knowledge of Judaism to their children. Yet, in public, and especially in church, their Christian conduct had to appear exemplary, and the need to avoid detection by anyone who might hand them over to the Inquisition often resulted in the abandonment of circumcision and the postponement of important feasts such as the Day of Atonement. As a result, knowledge of the Hebrew language and liturgy rapidly declined.

Judaisers

Many crypto-Jews, therefore, soon found themselves in an increasingly bewildering no-man's-land, one that in many ways resembled that of the many genuine *Conversos* who retained a dislike for pork and an attachment to various Jewish customs and traditions. For their part, the Inquisitors were now left with the unenviable task of differentiating between the two in order to put an effective stop to the ever-present danger of "Judaising". This was an impossibly difficult business, often requiring the prolonged imprisonment of innocent suspects, many of whom had been accused as a result of private jealousies and old vendettas and who were then further subjected to arbitrary questionings and torture sessions in order to confirm frequently unfounded allegations. It is, in fact, from these early years of Inquisitorial activity in Spain that most of the evidence to support its image for obscurantist bigotry and cruelty come from, and there is no denying that much of it goes a long way towards justifying opinions such as the one given by Samuel Usque, quoted in the beginning of this booklet.

Nevertheless, just as we saw in the case of the medieval Inquisition, it is too easy to dwell on the abuses, not least because the bulk of the information preserved in the Inquisitorial archives, by its very nature, readily lends itself to negative interpretations. It is rare to be reminded of cases such as that of Samuel Abulafia of Toledo, for example, who was arrested by the Inquisition in 1498 and acquitted of all charges. And yet Abulafia's case is more characteristic of the bulk of Inquisitorial cases at this time than the much better known cases of injustice and abuse. Indeed, the most infamous and maligned of all Grand Inquisitors, Tomás de Torquemada himself, produced an elaborate system of jurisprudence that was, in fact, far in advance of any other in contemporary Europe. His improvement of the quality of Inquisitorial prisons and prison food was so successfully carried out, that it soon became a recurring practice for prisoners of civil jails throughout the Hispanic World to blaspheme or pretend to be heretics so that they might be transferred to Inquisitorial quarters and be judged by Inquisitors rather than civil officers. So, too, Torquemada's *Ordenanzas* of 1484 were carefully planned to check the fanaticism and overzealousness that had rightly alarmed Pope Sixtus IV after the first few years of Inquisitorial activity in Spain. They stipulated that the membership and balance of the courts of the Inquisition should ensure efficiency and immunity from the most common sources of political corruption. Before any secret investigation could begin, for example, two witnesses of good repute needed to present the complaint in writing, signed under oath before a notary. Anonymous complaints were to be ignored, and any false accusations severely punished. Moreover, the instructions were careful to distinguish between three types of *Conversos*: those who had been born and raised as Christians; those who had been born and raised as Jews, but had converted in adulthood; and those who had converted in response to the expulsions. It is significant that the bulk of the trials concern the first type; the others were deemed to be "neophytes" and therefore treated with commensurate leniency.

It is, of course, true that Torquemada's *Ordenanzas* were not always observed. His successor, Fray Diego de Deza, for instance, seems to have been completely taken in by one of the worst of the Spanish Inquisitors, Diego Rodríguez de Lucero, an irascible character with a fanatical hatred of all Jews. Together with other Inquisitorial officials, Lucero soon began to claim that a pro-Jewish millenarian movement was spreading through Spain like wild fire. As a result, hundreds of suspects were arrested in the early 1500s, and Lucero did his utmost to burn as many of them as possible: 120 were burnt alive in one *auto de fé* in 1504, and twenty-seven in another in 1505. He would have burnt a further 160 in 1506, had not the new king of Castile, Philip the Handsome, personally intervened to prevent it. Thereafter, complaints mounted and Deza was forced to resign. He was replaced by the eminent Francisco Jiménez de Cisneros[10], the Franciscan Primate of Spain, Cardinal Archbishop of Toledo, who immediately began a careful purging of inquisitorial officials and managed to bring back the levels of measured moderation that Torquemada had envisaged.

---

[10] Although he is more commonly known in English as Ximenes, he will be referred to here as Cisneros.

Muslims and Moriscos

It is true that Cardinal Cisneros's record as a force for moderation had not always been quite so clear. He had in fact been the driving force behind the request to the Portuguese authorities in 1497 that they expel their Muslims alongside their Jews as a condition for the *infanta* Isabel to accept king Manuel's proposal of marriage. After this, it comes as no surprise to find that Cisneros was the key figure behind the drastic change of policy towards the Muslims of Granada after he visited the city with Ferdinand and Isabel in 1499. By then, seven years had elapsed since the Catholic monarchs had, on 2 January 1492, brought to an end over 700 years of Muslim occupation. Despite the ecstatic atmosphere that surrounded the event, the new situation could not avoid the difficult question of how deal with a large population of conquered Muslims in what was now ostensibly a unified Christian country.

Initially, the terms of surrender had been surprisingly magnanimous: Muslims were left in possession of their arms and property and they were left in complete freedom to practise their faith and observe their laws, to speak Arabic, to wear Arabic dress, and to uphold and enjoy their customs and traditions. Moreover, Muslims were to continue to be governed by their own local magistrates and no provision was made for them to pay any more taxes than they had paid before 1492. Nevertheless, it would soon become obvious that such apparent tolerance was, to a great extent, a response to the somewhat precarious position in which the Catholic monarchs found themselves during these years. The last thing they would have wanted at this time was to alienate a population that had actually welcomed them as liberators from the anarchy that had characterised the last years of Muslim rule under the Nasrids. Acutely sensitive to these circumstances, the first archbishop of Granada, Hernando de Talavera, wisely chose to pursue a policy of gentle assimilation from which he hoped that Spaniards, as much as Muslims, would find something to learn. He insisted that the conversion of Muslims should be brought about by preaching and careful instruction, which in turn made it necessary for Christian instructors to learn Arabic and to acquire a good understanding of Muslim culture.

Although Talavera's policy achieved some quite notable successes, it was never likely to receive long-term support. In fact, the conquest of Granada had created a clearly intractable problem by artificially dividing the hitherto unified civilisation of Islamic Spain and Islamic North Africa. Fears of treason and revolt were therefore ever-present, and this potentially dangerous situation made many of Talavera's colleagues

sharply critical of what they considered to be a
worryingly slow pace in the process of conversion. It was
precisely these groups that attracted the attention of
Cisneros during his visit in 1499, when he quickly
pushed Talavera aside and launched out on a policy of
forced conversions and baptisms *en masse*. The
predictable result was a rather disorganised Muslim
rebellion in the densely populated slopes of the Sierra
Nevada - the Alpujarras -, which was duly crushed by
Ferdinand's troops in the course of 1500. The event gave
Cisneros just the excuse he needed in order to deprive all
Muslims of the rights that had been guaranteed to them
in 1492. His argument was that, since the revolt of the
Alpujarras was an affront against the very sovereigns
that had generously granted them such rights, they had
now forfeited them and should, accordingly, either
abandon their customs and convert to Christianity, or
emigrate. Persuaded by the Cardinal, the Catholic
monarchs published a pragmatic in February 1502
ordering that all unconverted adult Muslims be expelled
from the peninsula.

In practice, however, the mass of the Muslim
population had little alternative but to stay. The general
feeling among them, moreover, was that the rights they
had been granted in 1492 had in fact been perfidiously
violated; and the result was that, although every

Muslim was now nominally a Christian - or, as converted Muslims were known, a *Morisco* - an overwhelming proportion chose to cling to their customs and traditional rites with a persistence now fed by a feeling of deep resentment. Thus the vast majority of *Moriscos* continued to speak only Arabic and to wear their traditional dress, and although a number of pragmatics were issued forbidding these practices, they were in fact never put into effect. Moreover, there seems to be substantial evidence, especially from plentiful documents in *Aljamiado* script (that is, Spanish written in Arabic characters), that a good proportion of *Moriscos* surreptitiously continued to practise Islam.

Tolerance towards *Moriscos*

In this context, it is rather surprising that the establishment of the Granada Inquisition, in 1526, did not result in any frenzied activity of arrests, trials and executions. Yet, until the middle of the sixteenth century, the Inquisition, in tune with the civil and ecclesiastical authorities in Andalusia, adopted a persistent attitude of relative tolerance towards *Moriscos*. To some extent this can be explained by the clear ability of *Moriscos* to dissemble, an ability that was not merely the result of centuries of contact with

Christians, but also of the considerable leeway in some aspects of Islamic legislation. To give but one example, a *fatwa*[11] in *Aljamiado* script, handed down in Oran in 1504 and widely circulated in Spain well into the 1560s, clearly stated that in certain circumstances Muslims might fulfil their religious obligations by attending Christian services, so long as their real intention was to worship Allah. Nevertheless, the Inquisition's relative inactivity during these years is perhaps more the result of the way in which it was held in check by the Captains-General of Andalusia, who feared that, if the *Moriscos* were despoiled by the Holy Office, they would not be able to pay the taxes that were needed to pay the troops.

A harder line

The situation began to change in the middle of the century, when a complex combination of factors began to weaken the power of the Captains-General. The Inquisition soon responded by intensifying its activities against *Moriscos* suspected of practising Islam. Moreover, the appointment of the conscientious reformer, Pedro Guerrero, as Archbishop of Granada in

---

[11] In view of the negative connotations that this term has come to acquire, it seems opportune to define it: "A decision on a point of Islamic law given by a *mufti*" (*The New Shorter Oxford English Dictionary*).

1546, marked a radical break with the neglectful acquiescence that had characterised the Andalusian clergy since the days of Talavera. In 1565, Guerrero summoned a provincial council to consider the implementation of the decrees of the Council of Trent, which had finally concluded its long deliberations in 1563. Although the provincial council responded with predictable lack of enthusiasm, it nonetheless gave warm support to Guerrero's recommendations, embodied in a pragmatic published on 1 January 1566, for the reform of *Morisco* customs. The pragmatic merely resumed earlier, unenforced decrees forbidding the use of Arabic and ordering *Moriscos* to wear Castilian dress; but this time the intention to enforce the reforms came in earnest, so, predictably, just as had happened in 1499, a second revolt in the region of the Alpujarras broke out in 1568.

Strategically, the revolt could not have come at a worse time. Andalusia and Castile had been drained of men by the levies for the Duke of Alba's army that had been sent north to crush the Dutch rebels. Moreover, by the time that the second revolt of the Alpujarras was finally crushed, in 1570, the advance of the Ottoman Turks in the Mediterranean posed a serious threat which was made incomparably more ominous by the presence of a potential, and deeply resentful, fifth column within the peninsula. The response of king Philip II was to order the dispersal of the Granada *Moriscos* throughout Castile, in order, he hoped, to bring about their assimilation.

This deeply traumatic operation was implemented with ruthless efficiency in the early 1570s, and there is no doubt that it brought a marked improvement in the military security of the Mediterranean coast of Spain during the difficult years of the build up to, and the aftermath of, the battle of Lepanto (1571). Nevertheless, it was obtained at the huge cost of creating a new and even more intractable *Morisco* problem for future generations. In particular, Philip's hope that scattering might facilitate assimilation was soon revealed to be not merely naïve but actually counterproductive; for it often led to the alienation of the hitherto acquiescent ex-Muslims that existed across the peninsula. In many old Castilian cities, for instance, the Inquisition seems to have reached a rather comfortable *modus vivendi* with the local population of ex-Muslims, notably through the use of a peculiar local tax known as the *situado*. Payment of this tax effectively ensured that the Inquisition would desist from pursuing investigations against suspected ex-Muslims, in exchange for a much-needed steady source of income. Yet, the displaced *Moriscos* that began to

arrive after 1570 were not required to pay the *situado*.
Additionally, perhaps because of the specific intention
to encourage their assimilation, it had been decided
that a special permission was needed before the
Inquisition could initiate any action against Granadan
Moriscos. So, instead of facilitating their assimilation,
this policy only led to the growing resentment of the
local ex-Muslims, many of whom began to ask to be
exempted from a tax that was now understandably
regarded as blatantly unfair.

The conflict led to antagonistic attitudes between
the Inquisition and a growing number of local ex-
Muslims. The process reached a high point in 1588,
with the burning at the stake of Hernando the
Barahona, in Valladolid, for "dogmatising".[12]
Moreover, although there are no records of any
dispersed *Moriscos* ever getting into trouble with the
Inquisition, there was a generalised opinion that they
were at the root of the disturbances. A special report of
the Inquisition of Ávila, for instance, written at the
request of the Crown in 1583, specifically explains
that, whereas before the arrival of the *Moriscos* from
Granada all the ex-Muslims seemed to have known

---

[12] This was the catchall charge used for those found to have been
preaching a faith other than Catholic Christianity.

their place and to have been generally subservient, they were now becoming increasingly assertive and difficult to control.

Expulsion of *Moriscos*

From a modern perspective it seems logical to ask why the manifest failure of the ill-conceived policy of forcible conversions was not duly acknowledged, leading to a situation in which Muslims could be accepted as fellow subjects. As we have seen, however, the unitary and theocratic conception of society that prevailed at the time would have made such a solution unthinkable. The *Morisco* problem, actually, was exactly the same as the *Converso* problem. There was in fact only one acceptable approach to the mounting tensions that grew more and more intractable towards the end of the sixteenth century: either the programmes of evangelisation should be intensified in order to ensure genuine conversions to Christianity, or the anomaly created by the presence of thousands of false converts within a Christian society should be eliminated by getting rid of them.

It was, unfortunately, the latter of these views that eventually prevailed, and a decree of expulsion was formally approved by king Philip III on 9 April 1609 - the very day, incidentally, that also saw the signing of a twelve-year truce with the Netherlands. This was by all accounts a rash decision, adopted as an easy solution in the face of a number of increasingly intractable popular and sectional pressures, but it was carried out with single-minded determination between 1609 and 1614. During these years, more than a quarter of a million *Moriscos*, born and bred in Spain and descendants of families who in many cases had lived there for nine centuries, were, at very short notice, with only those possessions they could carry with them, bundled on to ships and sent away to distant lands.

The Alumbrados

The unimaginably tragic end of the Spanish *Morisco* problem could hardly have been envisaged by Cardinal Cisneros. Indeed, the blind optimism with which he had implemented the policy of forced conversions after the first revolt of the Alpujarras, in the years after 1499, belied a trust in the power of sacramental baptism that, with hindsight, we may be justified for thinking quite naïve. Yet, it is clear that Cisneros, at the time, had no doubt that he had succeeded; so much so, in fact, that during his term as Inquisitor General the numbers of Inquisitorial convictions and "relaxations" diminished almost to insignificance. Moreover, as we have seen, the Inquisition remained largely inactive in relation to

Conversos and *Moriscos* during the following century, and it had nothing to do with the expulsions themselves. To many, in fact, it will have seemed as if the *Converso* and the *Morisco* problems had been resolved, and it is no accident that in the 1510s the Inquisition should have begun to turn its attention to other matters - notably the first cases of *Alumbrados* (literally, the "enlightened" ones) who began to be discovered at this time.

This movement favoured a type of spirituality that is often seen as having some affinity with the Northern European spiritual tradition known as the *devotio moderna* - whose most eloquent exponent was Thomas à Kempis, the author *The Imitation of Christ* -, a tradition that Cisneros himself had vigorously encouraged. But in fact the *Alumbrados* differed from this orthodox spiritual tradition in many fundamental respects. Their most alarming claim was that divine revelation was communicated by God directly to individuals. Those who heard this "inner voice" taught a type of contemplation where the human soul was deemed to lose its individuality to the point of annihilation. Thereafter, the *Alumbrados* sought to lose themselves in the infinite essence of the divinity until they reached a state of "perfection" where there was no sin and, therefore, no need for the Church or the sacraments.

In exposing and punishing this group, therefore, the Inquisition under Cisneros saw itself as a faithful successor of the medieval Inquisition's battle against the Cathars, which in the fourteenth century had been continued by Nicolas Eymeric in Aragon and Catalonia. Indeed, the Alumbrado doctrine that the highest perfection attainable consisted in the loss of individuality and the complete absorption in the divinity, would often manifest itself in attitudes that were almost identical to those that had characterised the Cathars. Not only did the *Alumbrados* claim that all external worship was superfluous, the reception of the sacraments useless, and sin impossible once a state of complete union with God had been attained, but many of them also began to claim that all carnal desires may be indulged, and other sinful actions committed freely, without "staining the soul".

The Inquisition under Cisneros dealt with the movement forcefully and decisively, but with none of the excesses or abuses that had marked the atrocious activities of Lucero. By the time of the accession of Charles of Ghent to the Spanish throne in 1517,[13] the movement seemed pretty much under control and the

---

[13] It should be noted that he was Charles I of Spain but became much more widely known as Charles V after his election as Holy Roman Emperor in 1519.

Inquisition grew largely acquiescent. It was in this climate that a group of *Conversos*, aware of the huge financial needs of the young king, offered Charles the tempting sum 800,000 ducats in exchange for implementing some "reforms" in the procedures of the Inquisition - most notably the need they saw to abolish secrecy and to reveal the names of any witnesses and delators. Cisneros, now in his eighties and feeling increasingly frail, wrote a forceful letter to Charles warning him about the serious dangers of any such "reforms". He explained that the procedures had been put in place specifically to prevent abuses and to secure justice, and that any changes would upset the careful balance that had been so laboriously achieved. Only recently, he informed the king, a *Converso* near Toledo had brutally stabbed his accuser after finding out his identity. If the publication of their names were allowed, he continued, all the abuses of the first years of Inquisitorial activity would return to plague Spain.

Cisneros could write with incontestable authority. During his term of office, blatant Inquisitorial abuses were practically unknown. Indeed, even in its very worst years, the numbers of condemnations and burnings at the stake were nowhere near the outrageous figures that subsequent propaganda would have us believe. The most authoritative estimates of recent historians for the years

1480-1520 (i.e., the worst period of Inquisitorial activity) range from the rather conservative 800 victims given by Tarsicio de Azcona, to the more realistic estimate of a maximum of 2000 victims given by Henry Kamen, with most other authoritative estimates opting for a figure in-between. When we consider the tens of thousands who died in the pogroms, it is easier to understand why some of the best minds in early modern Spain were firm supporters of the Inquisition. For even in its worst years, the aim of the Tribunal was generally not to oppress and to exclude, but to assimilate and to integrate; and the bulk of the population saw it not as an instrument of bigoted cruelty, but as an instigator of reform that would substitute a measured, judicial punishment of the guilty for the indiscriminate mob massacres of thousands of innocent people.

Still, it would be fatuous to attempt to play down the appalling tragedy of these dark years. No matter how much we try to understand the context, it is impossible to justify the attempt to coerce Jews and Muslims into accepting baptism. The justified resentment set up or confirmed in many Jewish and Muslim minds goes a long way towards explaining the enduring and worldwide consequences of the expulsions and their subsequent association with the injustices and abuses of the Inquisition. All this would receive further confirmation with the emergence of a very different, but in the end equally intractable, movement, one which ironically emerged just at the time when many Inquisitors in Spain might well have thought that their mission had been accomplished.

Protestantism

Cisneros died on 8 November 1517, a mere week after Martin Luther had nailed his ninety-five theses to the door of Wittenberg Cathedral. Years later, Charles V would have good reasons to thank the late Cardinal for his stern warning about "reforms" that would have rendered the Inquisition considerably less effective in the struggle against the movement that Luther had unleashed. For, although at the time of Cisneros's death Spain appeared to be firmly orthodox, there were plenty of intellectual and spiritual movements that would inevitably give cause for concern in the wake of the Lutheran revolt. Not least among them was the immense popularity of the works of Erasmus, whose sharp attacks on clerical abuses would be readily interpreted by Lutheran writers as veiled attacks on the rites and ceremonies of Catholicism and many of its dogmas.

With hindsight it is at first sight somewhat puzzling that Cisneros himself had been favourably disposed towards the writings of Erasmus, especially his

translations of the New Testament and his work on
Patristics. Moreover, two of Cisneros's immediate
successors - Alonso de Fonseca as Archbishop of
Toledo and Alonso Manrique as Inquisitor General -
were both keen enthusiasts of Erasmus; they even
championed a translation of the *Enchiridion*,
published in 1526, that became an immediate and
outstanding best seller. But, in fact, the popularity of
Erasmus in Spain at this time can be explained in very
much the same way as his popularity in humanist
circles across Europe. A key feature of his writings
was the way in which they fused into a single
intellectual tradition the main conflicting currents of
the late fifteenth century: the Netherlands piety of the
devotio moderna and the Windisheim reform
movement, Florentine neo-Platonism, humanistic
textual scholarship, and the various anxieties of a
growing "middle class" increasingly aware of its
needs and its potential for social action. In virtually
every one of these respects the Spain of Cisneros
anticipated and prefigured the Erasmian synthesis:
commercial contacts with Flanders had brought
marked Flemish influences to Castile; ties between
Italy and the Crown of Aragon had prepared the
ground for the dissemination of Italian humanism; the
introduction of the printing press in 1473 had helped

to popularise humanist learning by making classical texts widely available to the interested public; and the Italian-inspired humanism patronised by the court soon found keen adherents in urban areas, especially among the very groups that Isabel and Ferdinand had mostly relied upon during the civil war and the campaign against Granada, as well as in their efforts to offset the destabilising influence of an independent-minded aristocracy. As we have seen, among these groups *Conversos* were especially conspicuous.

Lutheranism

Before Lutheranism became a serious threat, it seemed as if all these movements would be successfully incorporated and assimilated into Spanish Catholic culture, even in official and orthodox circles. The keen "Erasmianism" of Fonseca and Manrique was matched by the support given to the movement by the court of Charles V. Indeed, between 1526 and 1535 the works of the sage of Rotterdam enjoyed such enormous popularity in Spain that it is impossible to find a comparable development in any other European country.

Nevertheless, it was inevitable that, in proportion as Lutheranism became more threatening, any movement of reform and criticism, however implicit, would be seen in a less favourable light. It is instructive, for example, to compare the treatment of the *Alumbrados* under Cisneros in the 1510s and under Marnique in the 1520s. Whereas Cisneros, as we have seen, was alarmed by the clear links he saw between *Alumbrado* doctrines and any remnants of Catharism, Manrique was more concerned to locate any hints of Lutheranism in the movement. Interestingly, Manrique himself fell into disfavour among traditionalists after Charles V left Spain for Italy in 1529, taking with him some of the most influential Erasmians, and was thereafter confined to his see of Seville. The links between Erasmus and Luther were now all too blatant to anyone with an interest in locating heresy, particularly when it became increasingly clear that the large majority of those found to be implicated in suspected heterodox activities, be they mystical, Erasmian or Lutheran, also happened to be *Conversos*. Could it be that the *Converso* problem had not, after all, been resolved?

The situation naturally bred enormous tension and suspicion. During the early 1530s, a good number of distinguished intellectuals who had been favoured by Cisneros were imprisoned by the Inquisition on suspicion of Lutheranism. The most notorious of these was the distinguished Erasmian Juan de Vergara, one of the best classical scholars of his generation, who had collaborated closely with Cisneros in the preparation of the Polyglot bible. The tide seemed quite definitively to have turned against Erasmus, and it must be admitted that in some respects the suspicions were justified; for various Protestants did in fact emerge from formerly *Alumbrado* circles after adapting Erasmian opinions that moved them in the direction of Luther's doctrine of justification by faith alone. But it would take another full generation before Lutheranism began to take root in Spain. Before 1558, fewer than fifty people were arrested by the Inquisition on suspicion of Lutheranism, and most of them were released after abjuring "errors" that were difficult to identify as specifically Protestant. But in 1557 substantial groups of Protestants were exposed in Seville and Valladolid, an event that sent shock waves across the peninsula.

Suppression of Protestantism

By this time Charles V had abdicated in favour of his son Philip and had retired to the monastery of Yuste in Extremadura. As soon as he heard the news, however, he penned a famous letter to his daughter Juana, who was serving as regent during Philip II's absence in the Netherlands, urging her to show no mercy in the suppression of the movement. The letter is especially significant when we remember that Charles had spent a good part of his reign hoping, and indeed trying, to heal the split with Protestantism in his role as Holy Roman Emperor. It was only after the failure of the religious colloquy at Regensburg, in 1541, that Charles began to resign himself to the fact that any hopes for reunification were unrealistic. From his retirement in Yuste, he will no doubt have looked back on these years with deep regret at not having done more to nip the Protestant "cancer" in the bud, adamant that the same kind of mistake should under no circumstances be allowed in Spain. "Believe me", he concluded in his letter to Juana, "if so great an evil is not suppressed and remedied without distinction of persons from the very beginning, I cannot promise that the king or anyone else will be in a position to do it afterwards".[14]

Juana need not have worried too much on that front. Even as Charles was writing to her, the Inquisitor General, Fernando de Valdés, had begun a series of arrests that would confirm him in his opinion that it would be a dreadful mistake to treat Protestants with the leniency that had come to characterise the Inquisition since the time of Cisneros. Up until then, he argued, most of those accused had been ignorant, or deluded, or confused; but the Protestants were intelligent, educated, well connected and, thus, extremely dangerous.

---

[14] Quoted by Kamen, *op. cit.* p. 95.

Auto de Fé

The result was a series of *autos de fé* in Valladolid and Seville that effectively wiped out Protestantism in Spain. The seriousness with which the threat was taken can be seen in the notorious arrest of none other than the primate of the Spanish Church, Bartolomé Carranza de Miranda, Archbishop of Toledo and close confidant of king Philip II, who became a suspect after a number of Protestants claimed to have been influenced by his writings. Among those affected were also a large number of foreigners, a few of whom were burnt, while many others received harsh punishments, including being sent to the galleys. It is from these years that the infamy of the Spanish Inquisition began to spread across Protestant Europe, only to be reinforced by a successful international network of Jews, many of whom had settled in Amsterdam at a time when the relations between Spain and the Netherlands were reaching their lowest ebb. In the new circumstances it is not difficult to understand how the bitter memories of the tragic expulsion of 1492 were revived and combined with stories of Protestant suffering at the hands of the Spanish Inquisition, to contribute to the formation of the anti-Spanish "Black Legend" that even nowadays seems irresistibly persuasive.

And yet, in perspective, the Protestant crisis in Spain seems decidedly tame when compared with the history of religious persecution elsewhere at this time. Between 1559 and 1566 the Spanish Inquisition condemned just over a hundred convicted Protestants to be burnt at the stake; the French under Henry II burnt at least twice and the English under Mary at least three times as many. Besides, it is acutely ironic that the Spanish Inquisition should have become so closely associated with the unpleasant reality of torture, when, in fact, no other judicial institution in the early modern period did more to mitigate torture and to bring it under control. As for its association with obscurantist bigotry, it should be remembered that Spain was the one area of Western Europe to have been spared the witch craze, and that this was in no small measure due to the Inquisition's careful handling of the phenomenon. While in the rest of Western Europe tens of thousands of witches were being sent to the stake, no witches were burnt in Spain. Notably, during an episode of witch panic in the Basque country that looked in danger of getting out of hand in 1610, the local Inquisitor, Alonso de Salazar y Frías, conducted a meticulous investigation, isolating numerous suspects and taking them, one by one, to the sites of the alleged Sabbats. After comparing their stories, he concluded that none of the accusations could be proved; in the process he earned himself the name "the witches' advocate". It must be admitted that such a conscientious and measured approach was simply inconceivable in any other contemporary court of justice.

Nor is the Spanish Inquisition's reputation for intellectual narrow-mindedness in the least justified. It is worth remarking that no intellectual was ever burnt in Spain, and that, throughout the sixteenth and seventeenth centuries, Spanish Inquisitors generally retained a measure of sanity, moderation and balance scarcely to be found elsewhere in Europe. The Copernican system, for instance, was not merely approved by Spanish Inquisitors but positively recommended in Spanish universities, so much so that Galileo briefly considered moving to Spain shortly before his problems with the Roman Inquisition began. And at the time when English and French monarchs had begun to claim absolute power, not only over the State, but also over the Church, the Spanish Inquisitors made a point of rebuking the king's confessor for preaching in favour of the absolute power of the King. Yet, generations of children have been taught to contrast the freedom of England and France with the despotic tyranny of Spain during these years; and, up until the early years of the twentieth century, thumbscrews used to torture Catholic priests during the reign of Elizabeth I were on display in the Tower of London as instruments allegedly used by Spanish Inquisitors.

Conclusion

After this brief historical survey, it would be impossible to deny that the Church has at various stages in her history been directly implicated in religious violence and persecution, and that the history of the Inquisition provides ample evidence of this. On the other hand, it is also clear that the widely accepted image of the Inquisition as an unacceptable instrument of power, bent on the maintenance and propagation of ignorance, superstition and obscurantism through the indiscriminate use of cruelty and torture, is not merely misleading but fundamentally mistaken. As we have seen, more often than not, the Inquisition compares quite favourably with other mechanisms of justice and social control, not least some that are still used nowadays in ostensibly secular, and even liberal and democratic states. Would even the worst Inquisitors, we might legitimately ask ourselves, have tolerated the indiscriminate imprisonment of suspects of terrorism in Guantánamo by the government of the United States?

It is, of course, true that, if the Inquisition is judged from the modern perspective, where the separation of Church and State, and the legitimacy and autonomy of secular institutions are taken for granted, it cannot but be condemned outright as an unjustified affront on the inviolable rights of the individual conscience. But if it is assessed in its contemporary context, where the conception of society was unitary and theocratic, the Inquisition, with all its faults and shortcomings, can begin to be understood as a genuine, and often quite successful, attempt to secure justice.

Of course, there is the opposite danger of using history as an exercise in apologetics - of covering up scandals and embarrassments in order to safeguard the good name of the Church. This temptation is to be resisted at all costs. A whitewash of the Inquisition would be as unhelpful and dishonest as its propagandistic denigration. No matter how understandable certain developments might appear to the historian when placed in their contemporary contexts, the simple fact remains that the truth and its moral requirements always have a value. It is for this simple reason that Pope John Paul II was perfectly justified in asking that, to mark the millennium, the Church "should kneel before God and implore forgiveness for the past and present sins of her sons and daughters".[15] Among these sins, he specifically singled out the many instances in the Church's past when the use of force and coercion

---

[15] *Incarnationis mysterium* (Bull of Indiction of the Great Jubilee of 2000, 29 November 1998), 11.

has been justified in the service of truth. "The request for forgiveness", he said, "applies to whatever should have been done or was passed over in silence because of weakness or bad judgement, to what was done or said hesitantly or inappropriately".[16]

It is obvious that any such exercise would be radically incomplete without first establishing the historical truth as far and as accurately as it is possible. Only thus will it be possible to reach an understanding that is capable of avoiding the mythical distortions that still plague our memory, so that, as Pope John Paul II put it, "from these painful moments of the past a lesson can be drawn for the future, leading all Christians to adhere fully to the sublime principle stated by the Council: 'The truth cannot impose itself except by virtue of its own truth, as it wins over the mind with both gentleness and power'".[17]

Upholding the Truth

The real challenge for Christians in the current intellectual climate, therefore, is precisely this need to defend and uphold the truth. For there is a widespread

---

[16] *General Audience Discourse* of 1 September 1999, in *L'Osservatore Romano*, English edn, 8 September 1999, p. 7.
[17] *Tertio Millennio Adveniente*, 35. The citation from the Second Vatican Council if from *Dignitatis humanae*, 1.

and very persuasive opinion, one which emerged with particular force in the various critical media reactions to Pope John Paul II's initiative, that a firm belief in the truth can constitute an affront on tolerance, peace and mutual respect. The fundamental value of the modern world seems to be freedom. Therefore, anything that conflicts with freedom, or that threatens to restrict it in any way, is immediately stigmatised as a relic of archaic prohibitions and "taboos" that the modern world has superseded. As Pope Benedict XVI once put it, in the scale of values of the modern world, "to live a life worthy of humanity, freedom seems to be the truly fundamental value". The notion of truth, on the other hand, "we greet rather with some suspicion: we recall...how often the claim to truth ... has been the means of limiting freedom".[18]

This is a philosophical rather than a historical question. Since it seems imperative to address it here, I have chosen to defer to the authority of one of the most distinguished Catholic philosophers of the last century, Jacques Maritain, who addressed this very issue with great lucidity in a lecture given at Princeton University in 1957. Talking about the problem of truth, what

---

[18] Joseph Ratzinger, *Truth and Tolerance: Christian Belief and World Religions*, trans. H. Taylor, (San Francisco, 2004), p. 231.

Maritain called the "error" of those who would like to impose truth by coercion can be applied to many of the attitudes that we have observed in the history of the Inquisition. This "error" consists in shifting the right feelings about the *object* (that is, whatever is perceived as true) from the *object* to the *subject*. This leads to the false conclusion that, just as error has no rights of its own and should be banished from the mind, so whatever is in error, including human beings, should be banished from human society.

The modern world is perfectly justified in its revolt against this false logic; but in the process it seems to have fallen into the equally fatal "error" of shifting the right feelings about the *subject* (that is, the person who must be respected regardless of his or her views) from the *subject* to the *object*. This is how the modern world has enthroned relativism (and, with relativism, also doubt, and even ignorance) as necessary prerequisites for mutual tolerance and freedom. But this false attempt to combat the recurring human tendency to intolerance and fanaticism by denying the importance of truth is simply a disguised, and far more dangerous form of intolerance and fanaticism that, as Maritain put it, deprives human beings and the human intellect of "the very act in which consists both man's dignity and reason for living" - that is, "adherence to the truth".[19]

The love of truth, therefore, must be at the centre of any reassessment of the history of the Church's involvement in violence and persecution. Any denial or deliberate ignorance of the truth is in fact a betrayal of humanity, which can never lead to genuine tolerance or mutual respect. To quote Maritain again, "genuine human fellowship is not jeopardised - quite the contrary! - it is fostered by zeal for truth, *if only love is there*".[20] It was precisely as an acknowledgement of the numerous shameful instances in the history of the Church when the zeal for truth has been separated from love, that pope John Paul II took the bold initiative to apologise for the Inquisition. The clear note of shame that accompanied the apology should be enough to satisfy those critics, like Carlo Ginzburg, who argued that the Pope's initiative was an evasion of responsibility. But even those who criticised the initiative from the opposite perspective, arguing that it was a naïve capitulation to the dangerous view that the world's "structural sin" also operates within the Church, should find some sense of reassurance in the knowledge that such instances have not been

---

[19] *Truth and Human Fellowship* (Princeton, NJ, 1957), pp. 9-10.
[20] *Ibid.*, p. 32 (my emphasis).

overwhelmingly characteristic, and that even the Inquisition, for most of its long history, never quite lost sight of the fundamental Christian principle that the truth can never be separated from love, for, in the last analysis, they are one and the same thing.

The Reformation in England

The events of the 'Reformation' led to centuries of bitter theological disputes, wars, persecutions and power struggles, and its consequences endure to this day. This booklet looks at the events which led up to the Reformation in Europe, and particularly in Britain. It shows how much that was good was lost in this conflict.

CTS Concise Histories reveal the truth behind some of the most important and controversial events in the Church's history.

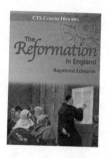

ISBN: 1 86082 385 8

CTS Code: H 505

The Crusades

Recent world events, in particular the struggle against Islamic terrorism, have seen the word 'Crusade' appear in political rhetoric on both sides of the debate. Yet how much do we truly understand these medieval wars? This booklet looks at modern popular conceptions of the crusades and compares them with the aims and motivations of those who took part. There is also a timeline detailing the major events of this notorious period.

CTS Concise Histories reveal the truth behind some of the most important and controversial events in the Church's history.

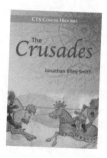

ISBN: 978 1 86082 378 7

CTS Code: H 503